Facilitating a Comeback

I0190592

A Discussion Guide and Companion Resource for The Comeback

By Betsy Muller

Facilitating a Comeback

A Discussion Guide and Companion Resource for
The Comeback - An Energy Makeover™ Love Story

By Betsy Muller Copyright 2019

Energy Makeover™ is a registered trademark of The Indigo Connection LLC.

Cover Design and graphic assistance by George R. Muller
Editing and layout by Holly Matson

ISBN: 978-1-7330482-3-1

Introduction

After going through many months of trauma, rehabilitation, recovery and returning to new routines, it became evident that I had a story to share as well as wisdom gained from a life-changing experience. There were so many moments that I wished there would have been someone handy to help me with many of the issues I faced with my husband along the way.

Early readers who experienced waves of emotion while reading The Comeback told me the book stirred up many questions. They saw benefit to further discussion with others. Those already part of a book club also liked the idea of having a guide would helpful for reading as a group. This discussion guide is intended to help readers to retain key points as they personally contemplate how to prepare for life's inevitable challenges.

There are questions for each main section of the book, as well as specific topic - related questions specific to marriage, relationships, spirituality, finances, travel, insurance, integrative medicine, self-care, brain health and ethics for caring professionals.

Remember that connecting with others to work through your fears and worries is a powerful way to neutralize trauma and gain support. This is the first step toward true healing.

Warmly,

Betsy Muller

Part 1 – From Bliss to Trauma

What do you come to understand about Betsy and George's relationship and marriage? How was the strength of their relationship supportive as the drama unfolded?

Do you believe in reincarnation or soul recognition? In what ways have soul connections made themselves apparent in your experience?

How could the initial ER and hospital intake experience have been made less traumatizing for Betsy? What events were most helpful and comforting? What was most traumatic?

Trauma can be characterized by the acronym UDIN which stands for
- Unexpected
- Drama/Death
- Isolation
- No Plan.

During the initial event and the early days of George's care, can you identify moments that had the potential as traumatic memories for Betsy and others?

How many miraculous or positive coincidences can you identify in part one? Which stand out as most significant?

Knowing that you only have 6-7 minutes after cardiac arrest to save a life and a brain by using CPR, does that change your view about acting as a first responder? Discuss your perspective.

Can you name at least 3 public places where you have spotted an automatic external defibrillator (AED) in the past 90 days? Considering the demographics of your community, do you think more are needed? If they were inexpensive, would you want one in your home? How much would you be willing to pay?

What are some thoughtful actions you could offer to a family going through a serious health crisis? If you've been through one yourself, what was the most helpful?

Have you ever experienced telepathic communication with a loved one? How could this be helpful during a medical crisis that prevents verbal communication?

One of the most challenging issues during a medical emergency involves privacy and confidentiality. What would you want others to share if you were in a serious medical situation, coma or unable to speak?

What resources are you aware of within hospitals and medical facilities to comfort patients and their families during highly stressful times? Have you used any of these services?

How could exercise, music or time spent in nature bring calm to a worried caregiver, family member, friend or spouse?

What role does faith and prayer play in the early pages of The Comeback? In what ways does Betsy demonstrate her faith? When is her faith most shaken?

There were early warnings that George had a heart problem before the June 10 event. What could have been done differently? Could this have been prevented?

Betsy shares her own challenges with foot surgery and recovery in the months before George's collapse. How was her injury and surgical recovery significant to the story?

What have you come to understand about emotional freedom techniques/ EFT/tapping and Betsy's daily self-care routine? If you were in the midst of a crisis, would you try this process? Which self-care processes are most appealing to you?

How is it that being told to keep a medical secret can be traumatic?

On page 32 you meet Gaisheda. Who is she and why is she important to the story?

Did George's family make the right decision when they decided to leave the ICU on June 15 and spend the day by the water in Saugatuck?

What are your impressions of Saugatuck as a destination? Have you been there?

How was selecting a hotel in the suburbs rather than near the urban hospital setting supportive for George's family?

What was the significance of the song, Unstoppable?

How were the events that took place on Father's Day significant to Betsy?

Do you have a will and medical power of attorney? Have you discussed medical directives for interventions such as feeding tubes and tracheostomies with your spouse? Does your spouse or family know how you would want your medical decisions handled?

What is the significance of the kiss on June 20?

Do you consider the Blue Dress a miracle or a coincidence?

One of the most critical decisions made after George regained consciousness was to move him immediately into a rehabilitation facility rather than a hospital. How was that supportive for recovery of his brain?

Part 2 – Rehabilitation

What significant changes and adjustments to life occur for Betsy and George as they returned home to Ohio?

What events on June 24 helped settle Betsy's worries about George's rehabilitation care?

Friends Scott and Mary invite Betsy, Mandy and Stephen to dinner at their home after the first full day back in Ohio. How was that helpful?

While George was in rehabilitation, he had many visitors and calls. How did he respond to them? From what areas of his life did they come? Who did he have the hardest time recognizing? If you were hospitalized, would visitors be important to you?

Betsy encounters many situations where she suddenly felt overwhelmed, especially around crowds and noise. What do you conclude about this? How did she eventually return to calm?

Throughout George's recovery, Betsy carefully invited energy healers to help George. What important considerations would determine whether you would integrate an alternative practitioner into a loved one's treatment plan? Would you discuss this with medical staff or discretely integrate on your own? Do you think Betsy's decision to integrate care made a difference in the outcome?

What rude awakening did Betsy receive on June 29? How did she handle the unpleasant news from the care team? How did the events of June 30 help her regain optimism?

Why do you think there was only one photo taken of George between June 10 and July 1?

How did Mentis/Neurorestorative surface as a solution for George and Betsy? What happened further support this facility as the best solution for George's recovery?

Part 3 – Transition to Mentis

How did George's move to Mentis in Stow create new challenges for Betsy?

What was George's experience as he began his stay at Mentis? What was difficult for him?

Betsy chose to take a few days of respite at her parent's cottage at the lake immediately after George's transfer to Mentis. What challenges occurred? Was getting away at this time a good decision?

In what ways was the neurological rehabilitation at Mentis different from the care George received during the previous 3 weeks in a general rehabilitation hospital?

Mentis allowed George passes to leave the facility under Betsy's supervision to dine out, visit health care providers and spend time at home. How was this helpful for his recovery and Betsy's confidence as a caregiver?

In August of 2017, about 60 days after George's emergency, the huge bills started rolling in. How was that traumatizing for Betsy? What resources emerged to eventually calms those worries?

What did you conclude about medical bills and health insurance from this story? How have you financially prepared for medical emergencies, health coverage for travel and long-term care?

What contributed to Betsy's decision to bring George home weeks earlier than the Mentis staff advised? Was this a good decision?

Part 4 – Adjusting, Trusting and Outpatient Therapy

How did George adjust to returning home? What were his biggest challenges during those first days back?

How did Betsy handle the homecoming? Was she wise to take a night away to attend her High School reunion just a day after George returned?

Does your local hospital offer a shuttle van for rehabilitation patients? How was that service helpful for George's recovery and for Betsy's ability to focus on her business?

How did Betsy navigate George's return to coaching? What challenges arose? How did Betsy test George's readiness for greater independence over time?

The opportunity for renewing their wedding vows surfaced after Betsy cancelled a training event scheduled in Sedona Arizona. How did trust allow the two of them create something better from an otherwise difficult situation?

What improvements in George's mental function occurred gradually between September and year-end 2017? Were you surprised that George was driving and approved to return to coaching by year end?

Part 5 – Living Well and Fully in 2018

Betsy and George chose to make the most of 2018 by combining work with generous travel breaks. Would you be more inclined to plan extra travel experiences after surviving a health crisis? How would you budget extra travel? Which places would you want to explore?

Are you CPR certified? Are others in your family? Have you checked your local resources or www.cpr.heart.org? Who would you invite to take a class with you?

Many life and business changes took place during 2018, including George's return to coaching, the sale of the Lakeside cottage and Betsy's need to find new locations for her spring retreat and monthly breakfast events. How did they handle these changes? What was most challenging? What pleasant surprises emerged?

George has an unexpected cardiac event after running a 5K in June 2018. Did this interfere with their plans? In what ways did this event serve them?

The couple took a celebratory Viking River Cruise to mark the anniversary of George's cardiac arrest and enjoyed a perfect vacation. What recommendations did they offer to other couples considering the Viking experience? For travel in general?

The Muller family planned a special trip to Saugatuck and Twin Oaks Inn to mark the anniversary of George's homecoming. What was significant about this plan? Who was part of the celebration? How did the group make the best of this reunion and vacation?

Concluding Questions

The Epilogue included both sad and mostly happy news as life continued for the Muller family. Was this a suitable way to end the story that continues to unfold?

What questions do you have for the author that the book didn't reveal?

Practitioner Ethics Questions

(applicable to EFT practitioners and those who professionally work with others as a therapist, counselor, coach or medical care team member)

Have you ever had your professional life interrupted by a traumatic event (unexpected, dramatic, isolating and did not know what to do next)? If yes, take a moment to reflect on how you responded at the time of the event, later that day and in the days that followed. What is your unique pattern of response when confronted with a traumatic situation?

What self-care processes would you apply for your own healing and balance if you were to suddenly be responding to news of a loved one's serious health crisis?

What considerations would guide your decision to take a leave, cancel or reschedule events, appointments and or professional commitments following a family or personal trauma? How would you know if you were clear and present enough to care for clients/patients? How would you determine when it might become unethical to continue working?

If you chose to take time off to respond to or recover from a traumatic event, how would you determine when to return to work?

If you knew a practitioner, trainer or supervisor was currently going through a significant traumatic event, how would you feel about having them in charge of your care or evaluation? What would you be looking for in their interactions or communication with you and attention to details?

Isolation is a very real hazard in the wake of traumatic events. What are some of the subtle signs of isolation that might be present for a healing professional after a personal trauma? Do you have any recollections of isolating behavior (yours or someone you know) after a trauma? What are some ways to reconnect an isolated person to a supportive network?

One of the precious gifts of surviving a traumatic event is the wisdom that emerges at a later time. How might going through a trauma offer positive transformation for a healing professional?

What kinds of wisdom have emerged through difficult events you have encountered in your work? How can gratitude play a greater role in the healing process for all involved?

Personal Notes

Personal Notes

Personal Notes

George and Betsy Muller intend to partner with organizations and groups to further the mission of promoting brain health, heart health, wellness, CPR training, AED technology and the use of Emotional Freedom Techniques and gentle approaches for healing emotional trauma. Betsy, George (and therapy dog Serena) are available for keynote presentations, workshops, public appearances and continuing education events for health professionals. Betsy's accredited training programs offer CE credit for many health professionals including nurses, social workers, chemical dependency counselors and therapists. Learn more at CreateandConnectBrilliantly.com.

Create&Connect
Brilliantly

www.ingramcontent.com/pod-product-compliance
Lightning Source LLC
Chambersburg PA
CBHW071803020426
42331CB00008B/2392